# New Humanism

## On the Path to a Humane Social System

Mohammed Djassemi

Bahram Jassemi

# Table of Contents

# Prologue

The purpose of this contribution to discussion is to draw the attention of our readers to the adversities and problems which make life difficult for people and prevent them from being happy.

But what is life and its true fulfillment? There are certainly many answers to this question. A brief summary of our answers will help you better understand the text to follow: For us the fulfillment of man's existence is achieved by consciously and modestly living in joy and love with a spirit of solidarity in the community and in harmony with nature! What is the main obstacle to putting into practice this, in itself, simple maxim for living a fulfilled life? It is the vulnerability of the capitalistic culture – a value system burdened by the hereditary scorn of humanity and hostility towards nature governing individuals as well as societies, not even hesitating to deprive capital, which is the result of useful work, of its productive and beneficial performance.

Our primary objective is put the capitalistic culture up for discussion at all social levels – regardless of race, nationality, creed, or other cultural or social differences – regionally and globally.

We hope that as a part of an era of the second Enlightenment intellectual currents as well as practical movements marked by new ways of living will result from this lively global analysis. Our hope is that this will serve as a germinating power for a peaceful transformation of existing relationships into a true Humane Social System. Our value concepts, ideals, and visions are depicted here under the term New Humanism. However, we, the New Humanists, do not consider this an ideology which is striving for power. It is rather an edifice of knowledge and wisdom from all peoples, open on all sides always ready to develop and able to grasp.

Mohammed Djassemi
Bahram Jassemi

# Introduction

A spectre is roaming the world: the specter of New Humanism. It is haunting every mind, every house, and every nation. Whether rich or poor, in the worldly metropolises or in the slums, Muslim or Christian – everyone senses that it cannot go on like this. Our estranged civilization presently ruled by capitalism has reached its end! It's only refuge is attack, which leads to incurable internal crises and along with it mountains of absurdity, more crass than ever.

The prophecies of Marx, according to which capitalists would inhibit the further development of productive forces, have not come true. Today's capitalism rapidly develops productive forces and constantly aims to increase output and profitability. Hence the innovative and productive side of capital is not the stumbling block. What is to be criticized and to reproach capital is the meaningless and soulless existence full of illusions it has endowed human society with in the form of a wasteful commodity economy, totally out of joint. Industrial production is probably what capitalism boasts most about. But its preconditions – the exploitation of raw materials and energy - have until now impoverished and polluted nature through enormous expenditure. And how will nature look in the future taking this ecological fact into account if industrial production in the world is not only not held at its present level but continues to increase? Disastrous without a doubt!

From a social point of view the consequences are just as devastating; at first people in their own countries are encouraged to subject themselves to consumption so that production can continue; secondly peoples who dispose of raw materials and energy or cheap labour are exploited and suppressed. The result: dependency of the people in their own countries on a rigorous dictate of consumption or on the banks - and colonial patronage combined with biased external trade.

Therefore the often praised "prosperity" of the capitalistic economy is not subject to a good omen; it is the fatal result of a sado-masochistic culture which encourages us to create the conditions for our own sufferings by raping nature and suppressing other peoples.

Apologists of the capitalistic system mystify mankind's existing world of experience, as L. D. Laing described it precisely long ago:

> It is not sufficient to destroy our own experience and that of others. You have to superimpose false awareness - used to its own falseness, according to Markuse – on this devastation. Exploitation

must not be regarded as such. It must be regarded as a charitable act (…). Colonial governors not only deceive the natives (Fanon); they are also bound to deceive themselves (…). In order to rationalize our warmongering industrial complex we are obliged to destroy our ability to see what is happening before our very own eyes.[1]

Mystification crowns perverse reality and celebrates it as a historical highlight worth being imitated and without an alternative. However, the internal contradictions of the system are repeatedly the cause of mankind's doubts. Here the question arises: "Will there ever be a way to escape? Somehow things must go on!"

Dominating universal capital lashes out like a wounded snake fighting massively all states not willing to take part, destroys the greatest achievement of the European Enlightenment, tears apart the Charter of the United Nations, ignores the law of nations, and is not reluctant to conquer the mineral resources of other peoples even by means of military occupation. Even within their own societies people become victims of the evils of the estranged regime; crises, unemployment, destruction of social rights, slavery to debt, excavation of democracy, pollution of the environment, criminality, discrimination against women, drugs, ethnical and religious resentment, extensive poverty, human alienation, loss of meaning, uncertainty about the future, uneasiness and discomfort, technomorphic behaviour, anonymity, loss of individuality, and the loneliness of people in a world where joy has vanished. The reactions to this world jolted by crises and disaster are varied:

> Let us begin with the apologists of the existing system. For them the world is all right and there is no alternative to capitalism. It is deemed the high point of history and the absolute optimum! Of course there is differentiation within this group; hawks here, doves there. The doves among the apologists of world capitalism have established the Reformer Party; with dots and cosmetic tricks they have created a gloss to cover the existing system. They assert: "Here in the West we are thriving. What do we care about the few lazybones at home and the millions who are starving out there? It's their own fault. Money lies in the streets. It's there for the taking!"
>
> The advocate party is confronted by the non-conformist party which expresses numerous internal nuances:

1) Religious fundamentalists are radical and inflexible. They want to return to the medieval, primitive beginnings and regard the old original communities of their religion as a divine order to yearn for and to be reinstated. It was a work of the devil which has lured the people from these divine original communities in order to spread its power in the present Western civilization and to lead mankind into decadence. Fundamentalists of all kinds tend to use violence and to destroy culture. At best they can only destroy but cannot reconstruct. It is true that the laws of the Bible, the laws of Moses and the laws of the Koran will not be sufficient to produce a genuine alternative to the capitalist system valid for the society as a whole. The result of their refusal of democracy and ignorance of the characteristics of capitalism is that the fight against capitalism remains verbal. In the end the fundamentalists themselves become its miserable victims.

   Thus the circle closes and the fundamentalists undergo a metamorphosis into "evil", their original enemy. At this point we, the New Humanists, are sure that an open dialogue, above all with the practising youth, is urgently necessary. Here we will most heartily engage ourselves for the sake of securing peace among the different religious directions and beliefs.

2) On the other hand, the "leftists" plead for socialism. They pretend that socialism is the only system promising mankind a light of hope in the dark future. However, past experience shows that socialism leads to bureaucratic state capitalism if you fail to liberate yourself from Cartesian rationalism, if you cling to technocratic materialism as a consequence, if you introduce a totally centralized economic system, and if you replace democracy and the free participation of citizens by the sole dominance of one party. Those socialists, however, who have learned from this bitter experience but have preserved their ideals, stand near to us, the New Humanists. Together with them we will take the path to a future humane order. In a certain sense New Humanism has emerged from the synthesis and constructive processing of socialist theory and practice.

3) We, the New Humanists, are striving for a Humane System leading us out of the present one. It will have a cultural,

social, economic, and political order yet to be developed. However, it will only develop as a consequence of a thorough and worldwide intellectual dispute. At the same time it will allow us to alter our way of life and to act with the civil society with the force of best practice. Therefore a second active Enlightenment will stand at the beginning. The first Enlightenment initiated the modern age, in which the freedom of man, his dignity, and his maturity were the focal points. However, the flaw of this époque was embedded in

    a. its Europe centricity and
    b. its rationalism.

New Humanism can only meet its own demands if it fully recognizes man as a genus and an individual. Hence the Enlightenment we advocate must seize mankind and be inspired and guided by wisdom, by the culture and the spirit of all peoples. Tolerance and openness are therefore the prerequisites of such a cultural encounter which will lead to the mutual processing and penetration of values; a gigantic task promising humanity undreamed-of perspectives for a peaceful and spiritual life. European rationalism must be corrected in respect to scientific methods as well as to its image of the world and mankind. Above all, the monstrous product of this rationalism – machinism and technocratic materialism – is liable for a great deal of the evil which has been delivered to the world by the Western civilization.

While the first Enlightenment has claimed to organize the world according to sensibility, we are striving for a New Humane System based on happiness. Therefore the well-known maxim of the first Enlightenment: "So act that you can will the maxim of your own conduct to be a universal law!" (I. Kant) now becomes: "So act that you can will the maxim of your own conduct to be a universal law for the fulfilment of your life in happiness!"

---

1-Roland D. Laing: Phänomenologie der Erfahrung; p. 50, Suhrkamp, 1969

9

Man is a spiritual being. If he wants to change something in his life, he must alter his attitude and his values. Social conditions cannot be changed before we change ourselves, our values, and our principles. The evolution of a Humane Social System will also be the result of a long lasting broad spiritual dispute. Hence a profound change of values will be achieved and new orders and structures will emerge. The change of values, it is true, will bring about a change in our way of living; we do not want to continue our old habits. We want to eliminate and push aside estranged and capitalistic and detrimental ways of living, idols, habits, targets, automatic agreements without reflection, cherished trivialities, and burdening fears. We want to turn to new values, targets, and ideals which will give our life new purpose and direction, a new substance and a real meaning. Therefore we are talking about "active enlightenment", because its process is not only theoretical but rather a practical demonstration of a new way of living.

The most detrimental, the most inhumane way of living presently governing not only the industrial nations but also the whole world is capitalism. The essence of this way of living is determined by business and addiction to profit. Something only has value if it promises profit. Otherwise it is null and void. If it's about doing business and making profit, everything is permitted: exploitation, suppression, tricks and manipulation, warfare, plundering the environment or even destroying the environment… In an attempt to sell their merchandise, people are made appendixes to the world of merchandise. Merchandise, which is man's product becomes his ruler, becomes a fetish which opposes him in hostility and determines his destiny like a foreign power. Money, as a means of payment, is even assigned an individual existence of its own: it is given a new interpretation as the purpose and target of all actions. The consequence is plutocracy: Not only are we ruled by money but the owners of money have the power to determine our destiny.

The capitalistic culture declares everything is "matter" that represents the object of economy, because only through this are we promised substantial profit, clear zeroes on our bank accounts, material property, etc. Those who have no money are either nobodies or inferior beings - "Untermenschen"! Therefore it seems "natural" that everybody has to participate in a vain race for money, even if nobody achieves anything more than a deep sigh!

But the sigh of the disappointed and deprived human masses the world over represents a tremendous source of energy encouraging us to alter the circumstances. Even capitalists cannot protect themselves efficiently against being degraded to the legions of losers of tomorrow. May this uncertainty sensitize them to our message. Also the defenders of the capitalistic order of values cannot close their eyes to the forthcoming disaster which will be brought about by the menacing collapse of the environment in the future. Alert consciences, alternative thinkers, non-conformists, invincible individuals who have not dedicated their souls to the magic of money are part of the favorable conditions mentioned above – which hopefully will provide us with inspiration for a new start.

We have learned from our mistakes in the past: not to empty the tub with the baby in it. What we are striving for is not the abolishment of capital but rather the abolishment of the capitalistic culture which is getting the human race down. Capital is constructive, innovative, and dynamic and can be of great economic advantage when combined with "living physical and spiritual work" provided that there is a broad social commitment, a fair distribution of property to the employees of the enterprises, and an unleashing from governmental power.

With our values, ideals, and principles we put forth alternatives to the value conceptions, ideals, and principles of the capitalist culture. We will live according to these principles ourselves and also fight for them – a peaceful fight without the use of violence! The reduction of patronization and the creation of non-violent relationships between people are inseparably connected to the repertoire we esteem. Which values, ideals, and targets shall be the guidelines of our way of living enabling us to establish a Humane Social System? In the following we will briefly deal with these questions? Ervin Laszlo mentions three basic universal values to cope with the crises or, as he calls it, "the problems of the world: life, progress, and justice. " We need a basic transformation of our personal value concepts and efforts, a profound transformation of our laggard culture and an intensification of our collective political will."[1]

Based upon the needs of our time, we have extended these values and also planned other modifications.

---

1 – Ervin Laslo : *Die inneren Grenzen der Menschenheit*, pp.110-111

With reference to the first Enlightenment L. Feuerbach demanded "to convert the people from theologians to anthropologists, from theophiles to philanthropists, from candidates of the world beyond to students of this world, to free the self-assured citizens of the earth" by defining the way. Feuerbach's impact on other thinkers and scientists was enormous: Marx, Engels, and Freud, to mention only a few. Marx declared "the criticism of religion" for Germany to be essentially finished and proceeded to criticize the real circumstances. While Marx asserted that religion emerged as "the opium of the people" from the misery of social conditions, Freud viewed religion as a kind of "compulsion neurosis" which was to be based on a sense of guilt. For Freud, just as for Feuerbach, God was a projection that assumed the role of a father in heaven.

At the beginning of the twentieth century the Promethean man had now been fully created: a man who made many great achievements under the banner of reason and organized systems conform to the law - in medicine, chemistry, and above all in physics – the mother of the sciences. However, just there with the mother of the sciences, the image of the Promethean man suffered greatly due to Heisenberg's principle of blurriness. In other words, human reason could advance no further.

Now as new spirituality and the question about the sense and the feeling of the divine have become relevant, we must be careful not to let these questions force us to relapse into a new Middle Age. Problems such as alienation, isolation, and senselessness, which burden life – at least for Western people – also touch religion with their exterior edge. It is absolutely necessary that the contours of spirituality and religiousness become clearer through the exchange of experience, discussions, forums of experts, etc. so that dissenting religious groups cannot feint or dislodge real faith.[1]

Is *Philosophia perennis* in the right when it states that the numinose can be experienced personally? Does this provide the sense or meaning we are searching for? What relationships are there between us, actors in society, and the numinose from the core of existence?

As we proceed to a second Enlightenment, it is a must to discuss how the human soul is to be handled. As a mystery, as a gift of nature, as a present from heaven, or as psyche just as natural science has described it? How are we to regard ourselves as human beings?

Where does cognition of one's own self begin, where does it end and which paths may we take? What is genuine religiousness and what is genuine spiritualism[2]? To link man's acts to a "divine power" would be a relapse into the times before the first Enlightenment; not to answer the questions of genuine faith would be a continuation of alienating man by other means. The second Enlightenment must resolve this dilemma. The second Enlightenment must advocate the need of man for religiousness without approving the rule of clerical structures. Thus it must give new substance to faith which will be in accordance with ongoing holistic sciences. Two false opinions about the relationship between faith (religion) and reason (science) are currently governing people's minds:

a) Since faith cannot be explained rationally, it is impossible to reconcile reason with faith (e.g. as young Marx postulated.)

b) Science – reason - must be rejected because God's revelation – faith - is not in accordance with science (that is e.g. what today's fundamentalists postulate).

Both explain the incompatibility of faith and reason while making the same assertion, namely that rationale (reason, science) cannot be reconciled with the irrationale (religion, faith). Strictly speaking both points of view are established on the wrong image of man: One of them deems man to be a pure rational being whereas the other thinks that man is totally believing. But man is both a believing being and a reasonable being. Reason is one facet of the spirit; faith is another among many such as sentiment, vision, will, inspiration, fantasy, language, memory, etc. To reduce man to reason is just as serious a mistake as reducing him only to faith. In both cases the result is hostility outwards and impoverishment inwards. Man needs reason as well as faith.

Tolerance is something basically human. The theory of incompatibility being represented by both sides is therefore untenable because reason as well as belief is at home in the human spirit. However, both momentums in the spirit of man are able to learn and develop. But reason develops basically at another pace than belief; hence in the course of history we have recognized an "inequality of the substance of reason and faith". This inequality is equivalent to a law of nature. Consequently one day a conflict will arise between the sciences and some substances of faith. The diverging points of view stand up radically against each other at these historical crossroads. They mutually reject one another where it would be appropriate to adapt to each other anew.

In our times it has been and still is the technocratic materialistic rationalism which does not concede that faith has the right to exist. And, on the other hand, different fundamentalist streams radically reject reason and science in a generalizing way.

We, the New Humanists, would like to stress that knowledge does not eliminate faith and faith will not eliminate knowledge. We advocate the reconciliation of ratio and belief. In order to achieve that target we must, on the one hand, correct the deficiencies of the technocratic-materialistic rationalism of the West by means of the holistic doctrine and the handed-down cognitions of the East, and, on the other hand, we must advocate a reform and a new interpretation of the anachronistic substances of belief which do not allow adaptation to the natural sciences.

---

1. Edith Zündel: *Spirituelle Wege und transpersonale Psychologie*; Introduction

2. Georg Schmid: *Im Dschungel der neuen Religiosität*

The disappearance of the Divine from the world occurred in Europe in the 17th century and reached its climax with the French philosopher René Descartes. His scientific method begins with the statement *cognito* (I think). Hence existence is automatically divided into two parts: the thinking part (man) and the other part which is being thought (the existence, world). With his second statement *ego sum* (hence I am), existence is dependent on thinking or, to express this more exactly, existence is reduced to thinking. Descartes concludes that the essential characteristic of human nature lies in thinking and that everything which can be clearly thought is true. For Descartes thinking means to take problems apart in order to contemplate them in their logical order. This is his famous analytical method of thinking which has influenced science most profoundly and which has made it possible to achieve great technological progress. On the other hand, his method brought about the birth of reductionism. What is more, people believed that everything in the world could be understood through analysis, i.e. if existence and its aspects are reduced to dividable parts. A further even more profound result of Descartes' method of thinking is the division[1] of spirit and material. He describes it as *res cogitanes* (the thinking thing) and as *res extensa* (the extended thing): two areas separated from each other which do not unite. In this way he developed the idea of a huge world machine namely the universe where no life, no spirit, no meaning could be found. Thus the mechanistic image of the world was created and has been the prevalent paradigm of natural science for more than three hundred years. Even animals, plants, and the human body are parts of the world machine in this Cartesian image of the world pursuing their functions exactly according to a mathematical foundation.

Later on the Cartesian mathematical basis of a world machine was developed into a mechanistic conception of nature by Isaac Newton in which absolute space, absolute time and mass particles (material) are the main factors and are to function according to God-given predetermination. Its total function was like a huge cosmic machine. Newton created the idea of mechanistic determinism: everything in the world has a definitive reason and a definitive effect administered by a divine power – separated from existence - in a predefined form. Hence the world was reduced to a mechanical system.

Secularization of the world had already been predefined by Descartes. The belief in a rational solution to all human problems was now born and spread rapidly – also in philosophy. The mechanization of natural science was the basis for the justification of the manipulation of existence. Taking possession of and controlling nature were "officially" declared the aim of science, just as Francis Bacon had written. This ideal still appears today in the behaviour of the imperial man through the exploitation of nature and his taking everything into possession by means of force. We are all aware of the devastating results of this ideology: the impoverishment of nature, the pollution of our environment, consumption of natural resources, loss of hope for the future generations, etc. Measuring and quantification were also a part of mechanization: everything quantifiable was declared "reality". Correspondingly verifiable "reality" had to be recognized as "objective". Subject-object dualism is the fruit of Cartesianism which still prevails in natural science. When Erwin Schroedinger, a father of quantum mechanics, declared the barrier between subject and object as broken, he meant that this barrier did not exist at all.[2] Subject and object are one and the same.

In the next steps modern physics stated that all theories about natural phenomena and all "laws of nature" are only the products of human reason (*ratio*). According to Korzybski they are the conceptional map of reality and not reality itself (the territory). The quantum theory assumes the latter - namely that natural phenomena are parts of the chain of processes. The end of this chain lies in human awareness. If we try to understand the essence of nature – including oneself – through rational thinking (either-or logic), nature answers "paradoxically".[3]

Now how should new scientific methods look? In the following we would like to briefly mention four aspects of the new alternative paths to cognition.

Cognition-theoretical Aspect

Since Heisenberg's blurriness relation and Kurt Goedel's incompleteness theorem at the latest, it has become evident in the theory of natural science that everything that man observes is divided into two "conditions": an observer's condition and an observed condition. This means that something will always be lost or will not be observed. No system of observation can be created which observes itself during observation. Therefore Heisenberg and Goedel among others have described their theories as blurriness (in the material world) and/or incompleteness (in the mental world). You can also say that the unconscious of psychoanalysis demonstrates the same gap which can be found everywhere in the theory of cognition. In addition, observation is some sort of interference in the observed. Each effort to observe something of existence changes the matter observed. Hence an observer cannot experience "reality" but will always experience the result of his effort to observe when encountering existence.

## Awareness-theoretical Aspect

Understanding which remains inseparable from what it realizes became more than necessary in the 20th century. Before all other scientists the atomic physicists developed the idea that another cognition is necessary: an "intimate" non-dual direct cognition to intensify knowledge about the universe. Dual cognition of object-subject is necessary for practical life but is not absolute. Non-dual cognition is called Advaita (Advaita-Vedanta) in Hindu philosophy. This means that cognition, which is based on the separation of the recognizer and the recognized, is a product of an I-feeling different from the world. In other words a feeling which identifies itself with the universe and with existence recognizes everything as itself and thus as non-dual (Advaitic). Recognition has a strong relation to the I-feeling of man which has something to do with the picture (and the role) we ascribe to ourselves. Non-dual cognition then has a meaning different from that of dual cognition: absolute reality (Coomaraswamy, Ramana Maharashi). Resulting from this, non-dual cognition IS reality. Seen holistically (according to Huston Smith) reality is neither material nor mental, neither mechanistic nor vitalistic but rather awareness at the most profound level of the human soul. What is described by Mahayana-Buddhism as *schunyata* (emptiness) is reality which can also be regarded as the very first beginning of awareness (D. T. Suzuki).

The famous statement by Nagarjuna proves that language is not capable of describing reality (which we describe as the "whole"):

1. existence
2. non-existence
3. existence as well as non-existence
4. neither existence nor non-existence

According to Nagarjuna every statement about reality contradicts itself and reality does not contain separately existing things. Things (as well as pictures, thoughts, shapes) in their separate forms are products of our dualistic thinking. The clash of the new forms of cognition especially in quantum physics and the old traditions of humanity indicates that ways for a new paradigm have been found.

## Holistic Aspect

1. Existence is material.
2. Existence is not material but spirit.
3. Existence is material as well as spirit, i.e. rather what we pre-sense.
4. Existence is neither material nor spirit, i.e. in its truth it is something we do not have access to, resting in itself indifferently, no duality, no plurality, but a single unity.

If cognition restricts itself to existence being material, the result becomes a reduced materialistic view of the world and practically a technical world. Summarized the result is technocratic materialism from which a certain civilization arises. The West has produced this civilization. Former Socialism was also essentially based on the same scientific image. The statements "existence is not material but spirit" and "existence is neither material nor spirit" are highly appropriate for philosophical and theological speculations addressing reason as well as faith. But these statements lack the pragmatic component in contrast to the first statement. However, they quench the soul's thirst for a firm internal belief and for an internal search for the ultimate truth. Both are comprehensible from a human point of view because man does not live by bread alone. Luxury, consumption, wealth, power, and money are not capable of providing this satisfaction to the soul of man. While the so-called Cartesian scientific image belonging to the West is bound to the first statement, a holistic scientific image can emerge from the statement "existence is material as well as spirit", e.g. psychosomatic discipline in medicine. With the holistic scientific image and the corresponding soft technologies a new humane civilization can be set up.

## Ontological Aspect

Apparently existence is an endless process of creation limited neither by time nor space, an eternal new beginning and at the same time a new resurrection, a chaotic flow into void, an emanation of plurality from unity. Sensing this unity purifies the heart, leads thought to the essential, it allows us to believe internally and to do good, whereby in essence genuine religiousness germinates within the heart. Hence we perceive the one and only existence as divine: everything arises from it and returns to it. We could also express this according to the above Zen logic as follows: existence is at the same time divine and non-divine! In our words: reality is divine and divine is real! The divinity of existence manifests itself among others in its rational structures and lawful movements, in its chaotic freedom of decision to which we owe constant new creation, in its unsurpassable beauty, in its all-embracing principle of love and sympathy and in its mysteries never to be disclosed.

*

In an attempt to activate the Enlightenment for a Humane order of society, we build upon the following reflections and principles:

The holistic method commences with an understanding of the whole in order to better understand its parts. The reverse seeks to obtain, as an example, information about the character of a person from a cell in an isolated condition. But thus general orientation is lost if you abide by the single cognitions of science and lose sight of the identity of all existences. The holistic method does not completely reject the role of religions in human happiness – as did reason of the first Enlightenment. Apart from abusing power, religions play a certain role in the momentum of man's breaking away from the chains of a materialistic and mechanical system. We the people are a special part of the entire whole because it reflects itself in us like in a mirror. The internal encounter of the whole within us and the constant contact of the whole through us and our practical behavior make us gather experience and cognition which we depend on to secure our lives and the joy in our existence.

The whole motivates us by the "cunningness" of joy to approach it and recognize it and shows us the means and ways to cope with it and to liberate ourselves through the signal of suffering. Hence we the people contribute to our evolution as homo sapiens. Emerging from the stream of evolution many things have precipitated within us so that every person carries a secret book of cognition within themselves. We are to open this book and to make the registered legible. In the East an enormous treasure of such knowledge and practical directions to reach new spirituality or experience truth have been elaborated through millenniums. Likewise external nature is a book of knowledge where we can partake of cognition as we approach the whole.

Genuine cognition can be reached if we keep in mind the general relation between all things and phenomena in the world, if we see the bond of love which joins everything and forges them into a unity, hence if we do not strongly neglect complexity in the total reality by simplifying, superficial, and aggressive methods. One dimensionality and monocausality are the foes of genuine cognition. They reduce the voluptuous, complex tissue of liveliness to barren and scanty fragments of knowledge. Such knowledge is fragmentary, sterile, and not at all fertile.

In contrast the multicausal and polydimensional methods of cognition more likely fulfill the demands for total reality, whereby man is a participant of the whole.[4] The mechanistic way of observing reduces the world to a functioning machine. In spite of the achievements of quantum physics Newton's view of the world still governs many a mind indeed. Dualism per se governs many souls who yearn for the living whole.

\*

The whole is constantly one thing and another. It is permanently involved in a process of movement and development so that we can never pretend to know it. For all of a sudden it is again a new, another one. The universal system and harmony are repeatedly questioned by chaos in order to establish a yet another new system.[5] By means of dialectic understanding we try to live up to this fact. The unity which we believe to know constantly changes to another which we do not know. The negation of negation: unity splits into duality, from which a new unity arises. This process of development, this internal movement of things, makes the dialectic method inevitable. For everything seems to go through a process of development from the inside, whereby this development does not proceed in a straight line. Therefore the technical-mechanical approach to people and their society is not the right method to gain genuine cognition of mankind.

On the contrary it is deemed applicable to summon a spiritually growing understanding in order to grasp intricate, organically complex processes. Ontological reductionism degrades man as a kind of mammal to the level of the ape[6] and seeks to base man's anatomy on that of the ape. However, man is essentially a spirit-body nature. His development, his world and his fate take their course in a growing way. Effort to perceive this way by means of either-or logic or by the mechanical-technical procedure or by methods of natural science will fail. The human spirit does not remain constant as natural processes do: it rather obeys variable decisions of the free will which are influenced consciously or unconsciously by an order of values.

---

1- Werner Heisenberg, *Physik und Philosophie*, Stuttgart , 1972

2- Erwin Schroedinger, *Geist und Materie*, Braunschwieg, 1959

3- "Wenn die Bezogenheit der objektivierenden Naturerscheinung auf den Beobachter explizit berücksichtigt ist, ist Quantentheorie interpretierbar." (If the relation of the objectifying natural phenomenon is observed in a way explicitly related to the observer, then the quantum theory is interpretable.)
Carl Friedrich von Weizsäcker, *Der Garten des Menschlichen*, Frankfurt, 1980

4- "... Das Universum ist ein teilnehmendes Universum..." (.. The universe is a participating universe...)
John Wheeler, *The Physicist's Conception of Nature* , Holland, 1973

5- According to Kitty Fergusson, this is a paradoxon: "..., dass Zufall und freie Wahl einerseits und Notwendigkeit andererseits inhärente Eigenschaften des Universums sind ..."
(Coincidence and free choice are, on the one hand, a necessity and, on the other hand, inherent properties of the universe...)
Kitty Fergusson, *Gott und die Gesetze des Universums*

6- Konrad Lorenz

Without love the holistic doctrine is not a humane doctrine. Love is one of the pillars on which the holistic theory is founded. In order to explain the role that love plays in this we must demonstrate its significance in human life, in a social as well as a metaphysical sense. The ways of regarding love are various: from Johannes Kreuz – Doctor Mysticus – and his festival of love to Rumi – the Sufi master – with his lamentation about separation from the beloved (God), understood as divine or mystic love, further on down to motherly love, erotic love, and patriotic love called "human love", etc. All that indicates how terribly important the element of love is in human life. In general, mystics know three kinds of love: divine love, spiritual love, and human love. Present day psychology speaks about parental love, erotic love, egoism, altruism, and divine love which are all linked to each other.[1] All great traditions of humanity recognize love as a very important characteristic of man without which man cannot lead a beautiful and harmonious life and cannot be happy. Furthermore, love represents a social element which reduces the existence and proliferation of the dominance of violence in society. In Mahayana Buddhism *prajana* (wisdom) produces love and together they both reach the great objective of life: the liberation of all beings from blindness[2].

Creative power arises from a harmony which cannot be achieved without love. This kind of love is not unilateral, one dimensional nor focused on an "object of love". It is an enlightenment flowing into all beings. It embraces not only mankind but "all" creatures, the whole being. Only in this way is *satori* (awaking to true reality, in Japanese) reached and *moksha* (liberty) implemented. The Buddhist experiences the momentum of the metaphysical, not only in times of meditation but rather he lives it continuously in a physical way. And he senses being in an uninterrupted condition of unity with the entire existence. For him every day life is the feeling of non-separation from the world, be it from stones, plants or human beings. This is wisdom – cognition which is complete and embraces mankind and all other creatures.

In the Christian agape the individual links himself to God through communion and attempts to re-establish the experiences of Jesus Christ in their most beautiful form. Love life in the community for the community is initiated here. Of course the target is theosis. *Unio mystica,* although it is a personal love experience, is also a person's way for the community. The unification of the soul and God does not take place in loneliness but rather it demands the participation of all individuals in the festival of the soul, and it seeks the participation of all beings. The objective is incarnation, i.e. God becoming Man. Experiencing incarnation without including all human beings is not a genuine experience. Here,too, we can confirm the existence of the element of cognition (*Scientia sacrata*), cognition which was later desecrated as a consequence of the first Enlightenment and which has disappeared almost completely since the nineteenth century.

Through the way of love the Sufi tries to reach a condition of perfection which includes holy cognition. For him life is full of joy as he  - having opened the invisible eye – can see the *signatura* (signs) of God in all living creatures. His path ultimately leads to a condition of *sakinah* (eternal peace) in which he has unified metaphysically with existence. The last condition thereafter is the unification with divine existence. This is the so-called *fana* (oneness). In everyday life the Sufi tries to reach cosmical reason (the absolute) beyond human ratio (the relative): Without loving God, people, and existence, the Sufi path is not accessible. This accessibility requires love as the first and the last condition. Seen ontologically love is the origin of existence. It is the essence of God and by that we are linked to the whole universe. That is why cognition is an intimate view of reality, which can only be achieved through a sense of unification and alliance, acting without violence and by humbleness towards existence.

Hence cognition through rational thinking is incomplete superficial knowledge about things having little to do with the true nature of existence. As Pascal expresses: Mathematics has its limits, namely "where the regime of love" begins, as the heart has its reasons which are unknown to ratio. It seems to be "unscientific" to speak about cognition which is closely linked to love.  However, in the holistic doctrine you cannot refer to cognition without talking about love. And this is "unscientific" considered from the standpoint of present day natural science because the latter is founded completely on the dualistic Cartesian image of the world designed to observe the world and existence as "objects" and to measure and verify them – without sentiment. Thereby the observer is to remain "objective", i.e. to step back as a "subject" from the object of observation and to attempt to intervene in the object if necessary, i.e. to change existence.

This behavior results from an invisible master-slave relationship to nature. Man regards himself as the master of nature and allows himself the right to do anything to it.  This behavior is also closely linked to the capitalistic point of view claiming that everything is permitted on the market if only it creates profit. Thus the Cartesian image of the world is ideal for the technological society and for capitalism resulting from it. It has arisen from a master-slave relationship whose roots can already be found in Descartes and his ingenious ideas of controlling nature. During the last centuries it has raped, looted and impoverished the earth, nature, and human beings in the true sense of those words. The secret of the intimate relationships between capitalism and Cartesian natural science lies hidden herein. No wonder these co-relations glorify, admire and amplify each other.

The best example of this is obvious: the global weapon industry, its "products", their applications, their targets, their profits and results. It is no coincidence that the jargon of the weapon industry includes the expression "mother of all bombs" instead of "mother earth". Here the weapon is admired and worshiped. Thus the visible instrument of the reign of violence has taken the place of the genuine mother – the earth. Millions of people work for the weapon – the new divinity. They design new techniques of murder, mass produce them and market them everywhere. They even provoke wars in order to increase the flow of profit, making it possible and necessary to produce new weapons, and so on and so forth. The image of the false god "weapon" is always with us, day and night, in the news, in movies, in advertisements, and it continuously reminds us who the new divinity is: the weapon! The monetary sums alone being invested for it annually could save a billion people in the world from starvation. But we refuse to take that path, since otherwise the master-slave relationship would collapse. And that, of course, must not happen!

The social spectrum of love is linked directly to the liberation of mankind from the dualistic master-slave relationship. If people accept that nature cannot be controlled, if they regard nature as an "object of observation" but respect it as the core of human existence and if they recognize themselves and their fellow men as voyagers aboard the ship, mother earth, traveling through the endlessness of the universe, they will realize that we are all equally entitled to joy and happiness and that no man and no system may control us.

Mother earth is a delicate, loving creature. She is not "material" or lifeless but alive and therefore she deserves love and respect. We must not see ourselves separated from her as the despotism of today requires of us. We must be aware that raping nature in the name of science (atomic explosions), in the name of industry and technology (contamination by poisonous chemicals), and in the name of consumption (nitrate contamination of the soil) will lead to the degradation and impoverishment of all mankind and our own extinction in the end. A loving behavior towards the earth is an indispensable attitude in the holistic doctrine. The falsified, dishonest separation of men by race, language, creed, etc., propagated day and night by the attorneys of despotism, is in reality nothing but the slandering of mankind. We have been made to believe that the differences between people resulting from the process of evolution is equivalent to the "separation" of people. They are a beautiful sign of the divine meant to be a present, a gift as an opportunity for mankind to unfold and develop – but by no means an excuse to distinguish men from each other by false criteria.

We, the New Humanists, seriously ask ourselves what, in the name of God, is going on in our world. We ask ourselves why aggression, hate, hostility, and ice-cold egoism are spreading like a disease instead of simple love flowing from the heart and why egoism poisons man from inside. What is the obstacle keeping our internal sources of love energy from stepping into the limelight and from changing human relationships into a scented rose garden?

In this short description we have shown the devastating influence which the dualistic principle of technocratic rationalism – here subject, there object  -  can impose on mankind. Furthermore, we have said that the mechanistic ideology  - the consequence of which the world and also its people are degraded to a machine - strongly supports diverse pathological technophile and technomorphical behaviors and obscures the radiant sun of love like sinister clouds. In addition, we have mentioned the capitalistic culture with its derivatives spreading an enormous amount of venom of individualism, the scattering and depersonalization of man, where people not only become estranged from each other but also from themselves. Further ingredients of this ideology as the original spirit of the ice cold profit maximization and the merciless struggle for market shares only permit one logic: sheer selfishness. They repress, yes, even scorn every human sentiment and thoughts of love as romantic sentimentalism! Those who want love must remove the preconditions for envy, anger and hatred. Love does not infer overlooking these circumstances. The Bible says, it is true, we must love our enemies. Right! For only an oceanic, wise love alone is capable of making the world worth living. However, loving the enemy also means altering the circumstances under which there are enemies at all!

The existing estranged systems are obviously suffering from a kind of schizophrenia: economic life is the domain of ferocious hyenas, where human life cannot survive. Here morals, love, friendship, gentleness, and nobility are out of place. Here you are either man – and confirm your doom – or you howl with the wolves and make a career. This separation divides life into diametrically opposite parts excluding each other: here love and devotion, there brutality and cold heartedness – the clinical picture of mankind in a world of estrangement and alienation. "And although everyone knows that human feelings such as love and devotion to others cannot be measured with money." [3] Above all children and youth suffer this depressing loss of integrity and personal equilibrium; the adults' world seems pathological and full of lies. In their families they are lacking either love or they regard love in view of the "naked facts" of reality as a fake game of their parents. No wonder that many young people separate sex from love in their disillusion, that they turn to drugs, that they regard the founding of a family with skepticism and are looking for surrogates in false gods. Even from this disaster the economy draws its profit and trains a growing instrumentalized staff of managers from the rows of disappointed youth exposed to a menacing future. This staff is expected to be capable of anything and to stop at nothing in the name of "efficiency". So if we want to help love win the battle, we must expand considerateness, solidarity, morals, altruism, and the categorical imperative to the area of economics and to liberate economics from the currently reigning dictatorship of the jungle.

---

1. Erich Fromm: *Die Kunst des Liebens*, Frankfort 1994. In this book Fromm also precisely describes the degradation of love in Western society and in connection with capitalism.

2. D.T. Suzuki: *Satori*, Bern, Munich, 1989.

3. Dalai Lama: *Mitgefühl and Weisheit*, Herder Verlag (publishing house).

# Joy as the Sense and Purpose of Man's Life

For centuries the general objectives of political systems have been "volonté générale", "Gemeinwohl" or simply "happiness". However, these terms are ambiguous, blurred, and vague and they mean something different to everyone. Therefore, our discussion about the New Humane Social System will begin with a definite and clear term everyone can understand: joy!

From Epicure to Khayyam and Hobbes and on to Holbach, every philosopher has spoken of joy in their own words and has celebrated it as the elixir (potion) of life. By nature all human beings are programmed for joy. All human acts are – directly or indirectly, consciously or unconsciously – aimed at achieving joy and/or staving misery. Man is activated by two inert tendencies: towards joy, away from misery! Human life is settled in the energy field of these two poles so that no optimistic doctrine of promise or, on the contrary, no pessimistic doctrine of misery corresponds to human reality. The one promises paradise on earth, the other bluntly declares that misery is the basic state of human existence (e.g. Buddhism). In order to defeat misery and achieve joy, by and by people have developed craftsmanship and spiritual skills. Hence art, engineering, and science have been born. Subsequently greater communities and national organizations have emerged to ensure and maximize the joys of their people and to minimize their sufferings. With this development man has practically created himself in a certain sense: his arts, his reason, his systems of justice and morals, his state organization, etc. are all serving the growth of joy and the decrease of misery. Thus man gradually rises from the level of pure physical and sensual joy to the level of the spiritual, whereby distinction from the realm of the animals has been essentially achieved. (When Marx abandoned the stand points of his youth, he made the "material forces of production" responsible for the development of society and hence the spiritual elements of historical developments were neglected!)

What awaits man? Which development is still probable? We cannot answer these questions with certainty. What is certain, however, is that the way has led from the vegetative to the animalic and from here to homo sapiens. Possibly we might go through an astral phase of development along this path, a level of spirituality not yet imagined. The Humane Social System we are pleading for takes this development into account. More consciously than ever, physical and, above all, spiritual joy must be the center of our individual and social activities. The quality of spiritual joy must be developed and made the general property of everyone by supplying them with a reasonable amount of physical joy (food, clothing, accommodation, medication) from their birth until their death.

Hence in history, neither a prefabricated, imaginary plan nor the automatism of "productive forces" has been effective but rather the spiritual motivation of people itself arising from joy and misery. Material productive forces are at best the objectivized results of man's struggle for the joys of existence and for the decrease of various existential miseries. Beginning with physical and sensual joys man acquires the means and conditions for their implementation whereby spiritual joys, the joy of beauty, of truth, and of the good gradually arise and continue to grow. Without the struggle against misery, there is no joy, without hope for joy there is no motivation to struggle against misery. In this way joy distinguishes itself from sheer fun (hedonism). Joy is not possible without the struggle to eliminate misery.

Labor, for example, means "accepting" suffering for the sake of joy. Also artistic and scientific creation does not differ from this principle: the joy of beauty and truth only follows great labor. If we understand human life as a way of being obliged to have and to hold and to maximize joy, it cannot be meaningless. Then joy indicates the direction as well as the target man is striving for. It can only be confirmed by speculation and belief if there is a "hidden" meaning behind this perceivable meaning. The concealed meaning cannot be recognized because we lack the means to perceive it (Kant).

However, he who needs joy in order to live, suffers from imperfection. Hence man is not autonomous like the gods. His joys take their course before a background of existential passion. On the scale of joy fulfillment and the overcoming of misery, a gauge has been created which classifies things into good and evil according to ethics. Existence is divine as well as non-divine. Good and evil appear only in the mutual relationships of people and in our relationship to nature: From nature comes life as well as death, illness as well as healing. "Good" is what makes our sense of life in joy possible and enhances it and "bad" or "evil" is what is detrimental to it.

And the social interactions of people follow the same rule. Here is the origin of ethical and moral values and assessments: "Evil" is what is harmful to our joys or what causes misery. Vice versa: "Good" is what enhances our joys and reduces and removes our sufferings. The difference between man and nature lies in the fact, it is true, that nature acts automatically under compulsion while people act with the freedom of choice. Nevertheless, people are not separated by any Chinese wall;

quite often seemingly evil processes have a good end and sometimes good intentions lead to a disastrous result. In the words of Lao-tse: "Happiness has its roots in misery, and misery is concealed in happiness." If we learn from the damage, from negative experience, the bad has served a good purpose. A child is born without sin and guilt; only later socially caused feelings of guilt emerge and raise our threshold of inhibition so that we do not incur harm to our fellow men nor deprive them of their joys. But only forgiveness can cope with guilt; only forgiveness creates peace. "An eye for an eye…" is, however, the language of those who sow hatred and exercise revenge. In the end the imperceptibility of existence settles the question of good and evil. Our scales of good and evil are not absolute. They are supplements to the endless universal whole so that we may survive and rise from the level of physical and sensual joys to the ranks of the spiritual.

We describe the universal whole – whatever it may be – as "divine" because it exists by itself, because it disposes of unlimited freedom in a self-sufficient and autonomous way, because it is the existing entity and the one and only being – creation and creator at one time and in one. We refer to it as follows: The whole is divine and the Divine is the universal whole! The divine whole has prepared us for joy as a special part of itself, through which we approach it in order to experience it over and over again and to exploit it on a path full of suffering. Unfortunately the flowers of cognition have thorns but for us it is worth taking these into account in order to seize the beautiful and scented flowers.

We exploit the whole through the execution of work, everyday experience, artistic creation, and scientific effort. We exploit the holy whole, also through the internal stations of spiritual migration aimed at completing unification with it. The latter, in deed, remains an individual process for the most part.

The Humane Social System referred to here is based on targeting joy. Society will have to take measures to provide every individual with a justified and optimal amount of zest for living. Maximizing this zest and simultaneously minimizing sufferings – this is the essence of the political task the Humane System has set up for itself. Not only is the state community questioned about a joyful conduct of life, but it is also and above all the concern of every individual. Leading life in a fulfilled way strongly implies that everyone is very aware of joy as the sense of life. Furthermore, it must be our way of living, not only living in joy every day in as far as possible but relieving others of their suffering as much as possible and creating joy with all feasible power. Genuine, flawless joy is almost always linked to the good; only psychopaths enjoy the misery of others. Individually we can do a great deal for ourselves and our well-being. Neither our fellow men nor – least of all - the state will assume responsibility for that. Mere breathing alone – says Saadi von Schiraz – provides us with two joys: amusement of the senses through inhaling and their refreshment through exhaling. Yoga, meditation, relaxation training, exercise, education, expansion of awareness, play, sport, and wit all help us to cope with diverse stress factors, to balance the body and the soul, to enjoy physical pleasure completely in order to reach the ever more beautiful joys of the spirit - thus to lead a fulfilled life. For life is a unique present which we should prove ourselves worthy of. To live in joy and to let live in joy, to accept one's own misery and not to ignore the misery of others – here lies the core of man's dignity!

The policy of the Humane Social System represents in this context the entirety of public actions aiming at securing and maximizing joy and at the same time minimizing the sufferings of the public. Here lies an essential difference to the new Machiavellian perception of estranged systems where the acquisition and the preservation of power are the targets of politics.

Power – says Master Eckhart – is evil. Striving for power for the sake of power perverts man as it fails to make joy the sense of life. When the wise men of all peoples search for "joy in the Lord" (Bible) in "nirvana", in "unification" and "unbecoming" in the divine beloved (mysticism), we have another reason to regard joy as the objective of all human action. Philosophers only reject reckless striving for joy, an unquenchable "thirst" for the pleasures of life, an insatiable hunger which is immediately followed by subsequent hunger (Hobbes). Assuming power through greediness is what wise men strongly denounce; otherwise they do not object to man's natural and elementary pleasures of life even if they themselves are searching for the ultimate joy in "the internal contemplation of holiness" and heading for this objective.

For the sagacious even the smallest happy sensual emotion is a sign of the divine essence of reality. If we follow these tracks consciously, we will partake of the experience of divinity. However, if we follow the path of the sage, the divine itself will visit us.

It is possible that we are accused of being superficial because we strive for pleasure as the sense of human life. But if we regard people in their real life, we are taught better: They live on joy, by joy and for joy! Breathing, eating, drinking, love, friendship, enjoying one's own children, the feeling of having done good and acted in a noble way, enjoying music and beautiful pictures, dancing, health, rest, presents, warm glances of gratefulness, hope, everything that constitutes life is the implementation of joy!

Some educational institutions and ideologies call themselves "profound" as they will not be satisfied with those simple human objectives. With various words and doctrines they try to illuminate human life in the world, which seeks its completion in joy. Mazdaism for example strives to make Ahoura Mazda finally triumph over Ahriman through the work of man. Probably inspired by this structure of thoughts, the Jews tend to an increased approval of the word by the soul. It is true "that everyone (soul) shall recognize itself, purify itself, complete itself, but not for the sake of itself, not for the sake of its worldly happiness, not even for the sake of its heavenly bliss but for the sake of the "works" to be fulfilled in God's world." [1]

"Works" in this context means the implementation of the task every individual is assigned to by the creator. Christianity has made the individual soul's salvation and the liberation linked to it the highest objective for the "sinner". The opinion that the world is simply a transition to the world beyond, simply a "house of sin and failure" is widespread in the Islamic countries. Through righteousness and virtues alone we are meant to gather supplies for the "house of sustainability". Buddhism reduces human life assuming that it **only** consists of misery which we can, however, defeat through enlightenment. A thought-worthy definition of joy is to be found in the following sentences:

Joy is liberation in giving, liberation in sputtering out of oneself. It is a sentiment man experiences with an act of creation. On the contrary, enjoyment (of desire) is a triumph of taking; taking without giving (…). A strong person lives in joy, however avoiding desire. For desire opposes his/her conviction. Only those persons are searching for enjoyment who suspect others of desiring their possessions and who think they must act alike. For strong creation is a process of giving, of giving birth, of self-producing, of liberation through giving. Every creature shares in creation and creates as well. Hence the world of creation is a world of joy (…).[2]

---

1 Martin Buber, *Der Weg der Menschen nach der Chassidischen Lehre*

2 Manuchehr Jamali, *Mit dem Weg zu den unmöglichen Fragen*, Persian text pp. 191-192

# Freedom

With the Enlightenment and the progressive implementation of democracies in many countries of the world, we have only dared a first step into the realm of freedom, the necessary subsequent steps are much more adventuresome, exciting, and, at the same time, more decisive. With the democracies of today the problem of freedom has not been solved at all, particularly since these democracies themselves are suffering from deficiencies, are in need of reforms and are even partially exercising an alibi function. Therefore, we must put freedom up for discussion as a central factor for the implementation of a Humane Social System and we must combat those forms of patronizing and repression which limit our freedom and even endanger it.

When asking if we should allow drives and desires to develop freely or to liberate ourselves from their ties, two contradictive opinions result: freedom from the power of drives and lust is a contrast to the (anarchistic) dream of striving for freedom in the full enjoyment of drives and desires. The first opinion has always seen it as an obstacle for the spiritual development of man, for his liberation from the ban of the physical world (having fallen into the sinister material from which man was to liberate himself by renunciation), for his internal peace and salvation. Slandering desires goes as far as attempting to extinguish the "animalic" completely and to exorcise the demonic. Psychologists regard the extreme renunciation of desires, above all sexual joy, as the reason for many neuroses although they are willing to acknowledge cultural achievements in a certain sense as the harnessing of drives. For – as argued – no culture would have been able to come into existence if we had wanted to fully enjoy the physical pleasures to the extreme.

On the other hand anarchists uphold the thesis that only the complete freedom of drives and desires – living in total physical joys – will allow an alternative culture to prosper. This extreme definition of freedom ignores the fact that nature itself sets up barriers against the total freedom of drives; these barriers stand before every social standardization. If we listen carefully to our own nature we realize where pleasure is still joy and where it begins to change into misery. Abiding by this measure of naturalness is commanded by reason. In addition, in the community each individual's use of drives and desires finds its limit.

As for cultural values, we tend to accept the golden mean as the rule of thumb: neither one extreme nor the other but a life in harmony and balance as far as possible between physical and spiritual joys would be ideal. It is true that we must critically regard rich nations and their tendency towards materialism, superficiality, meaningless abundance, a disproportional stressing of addiction to pleasure, the hollowing out of the meaning of life, while bitter destitution reigns over the poor peoples of the earth, apart from the excessive lives of the thin upper class. Here we plead for more prosperity which promises a fulfilled life in physical joys, while we warn against the materialistic loss of meaning in a society of consumption in the rich nations.

In the following we would like to draw attention to other forms of government which depress our world and which we urgently want to liberate ourselves from. A number of exterior forces limit the autonomy and self determination of people and peoples:
- imperial force
- bureaucratic force
- medial force
- capital force

Imperial force is exercised either by states or by multinationals who directly control peoples (markets). Present discussions about neo-liberalism refer to these facts. "Globalization" as a catchword comprises the strategy of the world's complete subordination to imperial force. The military lever is being used more and more as a supplement to political, diplomatic, and economic levers which remind us of the old colonial methods of "occupation militaire". With a monopoly of high-tech weapons the USA offers to function as a protective force for nations with weakened military potential. But this protective function may also be interpreted as neo-feudalism in international relationships.

Bureaucratic force expands worldwide at many sites and erodes the democratic systems of organization. Thus political parties and associations degrade themselves to instruments of power controlled by oligarchy. Not even the democratic state is spared the cancerous attack of bureaucracy which increasingly influences legislative and judicial power. In a certain sense bureaucracy is combined with excessive state control suffocating citizens through its pressure and burden, by its rules and patronizing.

Medial force is one of the most subtle and perfidious forms of control (latent control according to Johan Galtung) accompanying the galloping development of modern communication technologies. Capital is a dominating economical power in our world which has impacted the development of mankind fundamentally. However, a "capitalistic culture" has arisen from the merger of capital, politics and the media; this has jeopardized the sovereignty of the people and the freedom of mankind.

Belonging to this culture are the force of money (plutocracy) and the dictating power of goods over the consumers.

All four forces mentioned above are different versions of the same phenomenon of estrangement (Marx): As you know, if in fact capital is called the "crystallized work" of many people being accumulated in private hands, command over the "living work" of the real owners, i.e. the workers, is really an estrangement. If we regard money just as a means of exchange, its transfer into a power factor over its inventors is a sheer perversion of reality. The same applies to merchandise; merchandise is the product of the mental and manual work force of people. But if it becomes a false god and, just like money, forces us to worship it and to subject ourselves completely to it, we are also mistaken, in this case, as we regard reality upside down. Criticism of the "capitalistic culture" essentially including the four forms of human estrangement and its institutionalizing mentioned here therefore involves the liberation of mankind from this perverse reality, the contemplation of which is nothing but false consciousness.

Other forms of exterior forces in our world are the open and concealed dictatorships reigning in many countries on earth. To be mentioned in this context are:
- dictatorships by parties
- military dictatorships
- civil dictatorships

Above all those can be encountered in the developing countries of Asia, Africa, and Latin America, where the struggle for freedom focuses on efforts to introduce conditions imitating Western democracies. But in particular these conditions in the Western countries and societies are the center of our criticism today. Hence we must explain our critical stand points regarding the existing democracies in the West to those struggling for freedom so that they will not strive for anachronistic targets. Other patronizing forms which we attack in our struggle for freedom include a series of handed-down regimes. The theonomic regime or theocratic regime receives enormous support from the fundamentalists of all religions. Hindu, Christian, Jewish, and Islamic efforts aim at such patronizing forms. Very often these targets are coupled with violence and cultural "destructivism ". Just criticism of those who look into the future and fight for new freedom is made and cited in order to make people fully discredit modern times. The patriarchal regime, which is above all practiced against women, is one of the most widely spread evils causing anguish to almost half of humanity in an open or concealed way. We have to blame this tough inveterate regime on the fact that women's rights are violated everywhere and that equal rights remain almost a worthless book.

In many places we encounter feudal and semi-feudal forms of control inflicting above all those people living out in the country who are underprivileged anyway. The term "liberty" has been associated with private property at the latest since the time of Rousseau. To what extent does private property cause or include the deprivation of freedom for fellow men - that's what it is all about. However, long term experience with socialism and communism demonstrates that the nationalization of private property was not equivalent to the liberation of the people at all. A class of proprietors was only replaced by a new class of governing state and party bosses. They handled power in an even more concentrated manner without competitors, more totally and without any opportunity for genuine democratic control. We will refer to this issue later on under "Solidarism".

We plead for a participatory democracy of solidarism, where for the first time, full sovereignty of the people will become reality. In this democracy citizens will be equal and free from those classifying, personal, handed-down and structural forms of control mentioned. Solidarity completes competition as a counterpart and gives it the right direction and the meaning it has been lacking. The participatory element completes the right of codetermination, equal opportunity and influence with the broad participation of employees and workers in the possession of capital. With the gradual and successive abolishment of the above repressions, suppressions, and governing systems humanity achieves an incomparable degree of freedom of action as well as enjoy liberties suitable to the astral phase of their spiritual development.

In this phase we approach circumstances under which we accept the world for the first time instead of being taken in by it as in the past. This is the peak of human liberty - in the words of Hafiz: To be free of everything binding in the world! In a world where "freedom to do the feasible"[1] will not seduce us into becoming the ultimate slaves of what has been done. For this does not promise a future in freedom, not freedom in the future. Yes indeed, "with this freedom we have in freedom to do the feasible there will perhaps be no freedom in the future and perhaps no future at all. We can extinguish life and earth – and not only by means of the atomic bomb which is the clearest and most dreadful sign of the feasible but moreover by what we experience everywhere today as the environmental problem." (ibidem) Freedom to do the feasible – problem No. 1 of the future – urges us, the New Humanists, to draw pessimistic conclusions if you intend to bear your products like "a yoke on your own neck".

In particular, we would like to underline the following issues concerning the problems of freedom and subject them to a final discussion:

1) "Making" as an expression of the dualistic principle causes a double wrong; you make something to gain control over what you have made. *Ecce!* What you have made gains control over you! With that the assumption of Marx and today's technocrats becomes questionable, i.e. the assumption that namely the freedom of mankind is a consequence of automatism and technical development.

2) The masters of all mystic tendencies teach us that we attain liberty through an oceanic, limitless love – the All Love. For love liberates from hatred and aggression; it is peaceful and forgiving and strives for unity.

3) Zen Buddhism teaches that we can attain freedom of the spirit by surrendering the links to names and to the logical conclusions of the mind, as "the reason which makes it impossible for us to reach a penetrating recognition of the truth has its roots in the unreasonable search for a 'logical' explanation of things."[2]

4) The call for the spirit's freedom from drives and the "inferior" forces of the soul already took its course in the spiritual history of mankind in the beginnings of philosophical thinking and of pious belief. The peak of the hierarchy of the soul was reserved for reason which could assume its merited position when it liberated itself from the control of the "inferior parts of the soul" – a performance only to be achieved in a well organized state community. This issue remains an important topic today and is expressed in the theories of political leadership and of the modern management of multinationals.

5) One more aspect of the problematic issues of liberty has always been the relationship between mankind and the world. The scope of statements and opinions about these issues extends from the absolute acceptance of the world to the renunciation of the hermit world. We will refer to this in the chapter entitled "Modesty". At this point we will only mention the old issue of linking to the world today which expresses itself theoretically and in practice through alienation and estrangement theories, in the supremacy of money and merchandise, in the society of over abundance and in the wasting of natural resources.

---

1 Arno Baruzzi, *Die Zukunft der Feiheit*

2 D.T, Suzuki, *Die große Befreiung*, p. 79

# Justice

Humanity is so closely linked to justice that a Humane Social System without justice is hardly imaginable. Justice itself corresponds to the thought of justifying and understanding the inequality of people and peoples. On the whole five reasons for the development of the inequality of people have been analyzed in political thinking:

- The Greek philosophy of antiquity regarded reason as "human nature". The analysis of the soul resulted in a hierarchy of the parts of the soul. According to this it would be justified to acknowledge this "natural" condition. The just order of the *polis* would have to meet the requirements of the right order of the parts of the soul. Therefore those who have gold in their souls should assume the leadership in the state over those who have iron or copper in their souls. (Plato and Aristoteles)

- Established religions have had difficulties in justifying and explaining to their doubting followers the glaring disharmony and injustice in the world, plausibly and without contradiction taking into account the absolute justice of God.

Nevertheless, the tortured creature has found support in the doctrines of religion in order to complain about the heavy burden or even to hope for liberation. Buddhists and Hindus have completely accepted misery; the only way to free oneself from it and to reach salvation is to escape from the cycle of reincarnation.

- There are also thinkers who trace the roots of inequality and the injustice related to it back to violence. Out of the mixture of this "dogma" with Darwinism resulted so-called social Darwinism in the 19th century, according to which a "natural selection" and the "struggle for existence" would eliminate the weak and ensure the survival of the mighty. Eugenics and racism were only the natural consequences of these delusive dogmas.

- Rousseau regarded private property as the original sin which expelled us from paradise and caused injustice in the world through "mine" and "yours". Consequently many thinkers like Fergusson, Millar, Lorenz von Stein, and Marx regarded property as the origin of class differences, a part from the fact that they interpreted man's escape from the rotten peace of the original paradisiacal conditions (Schiller) as a positive step towards the further development of mankind.

Later on many other scientists countered with regard to the experiences of Communist countries that, if the roots of inequality of people lie in private property, then logically no social differences could exist in these countries, whereas facts indicate unambiguously that they really do (Dahrendorf). In consensus with many other thinkers Dahrendorf mentioned "prestige" as the source of thinking in classes and of the development of class differences.

- Marx, Engels (in Anti-Düring), von Stein and many other social scientists like Schmoller, Durkheim, Simmel, and Bücher consider the "division of work" to be the reason for social differentiation. (Marx considered private property as well as the division of work to be responsible for the emergence of classes.)

- The newest (not necessarily correct) versions find the basis for "upper" and "lower" classes within societies in the system of values. These values enjoy a social rank according to the enforcement guarantees they support. Hence social differentiation is unavoidable (Dahrendorf).

The brief depiction of a central value of human society – justice – and of what different philosophers and wise men consider to be unfair, shows that we cannot avoid a broad discussion about the reason for class differences and injustice in our world and how we can remove them. There is a tremendous amount of injustice that our present world is confronted with in spite of all the progress made in previous decades. They are an immense burden to the alert conscience of all people who think with humanity.

In the chapter entitled "Freedom" we mentioned several forms of rule; not only are they responsible for suppression and repression but also for flagrant injustice within societies as well as in relations between peoples and countries of this earth. Children are the most helpless creatures being exposed massively to poverty, violence, prostitution, drugs, etc.
Our youth are facing mountains of our debts, an existence without joy, without jobs or income and ruined nature which they have inherited from us.

To date spiritual work is still deemed superior to manual or physical work; still the work of farmers and laborers who provide for the substance of our life and its continuation is ranked "low" and "dirty".

There are people who easily earn within a minute what a laborer, a farmer or a simple employee earns for a month of hard work.

For the simple man on the street there is hardly any opportunity to complain about the injustice imposed on him by a millionaire, a big influential boss or a corporation. The machinery of star attorneys simply crushes such a daring "querulous person" in the marble palaces of justice.

There are millions of women who are being tortured, beaten and humiliated; women who deserve our protection, our care, and our love. There are billions of malnourished and sick people in addition to those who are kept in ignorance and thus doomed to a miserable existence on this earth, while the rich and the mighty take possession of their last property and natural resources without mercy through unjust trade.

This blacklist can be extended ad lib with innumerable cases of judicatory, retributive and distributive injustice. Here the New Humanists are not only bringing up an indictment but they are also making efforts to let justice reign through their own lifestyle and their own personal attitude. For if we all act in a just way we will discover a world where justice reigns, in which the virtue of justice will triumph over violence, tyranny, malice, and sheer egoism. But how can we act justly? Jamali's answer is one of the possible responses to this question: "Moderation is the root of respect for other people. For every life disposes of its own sphere which is to be respected. Only in moderation can this sphere of life be respected. Moderation itself is determined by the shame and fear of hurting the lives of others. Thus with the idea of moderation, shame and fear keep us from disrespecting inherent law and order (called dad or dath). Only the immoderate have neither fear nor do they feel shame when they disregard justice unscrupulously and inflict damage on other beings."[1]

1 Manuchehr Jamali, *ibidem*

# Modesty

Philosophers of all times have unanimously considered modesty to be fundamental and indispensable for the ethical and spiritual development of man. Not before man "separates" from externals and returns to himself, not before he liberates himself from worldly ties, can spiritual development take its course. According to certain perceptions of Pascal we can even see modesty based in ones very existence itself. Pascal postulates two infinities to which man, as a limited being, is confronted: the infinity of the vast and the infinity of the minute. The universe on the one hand as the limitless whole and the tiniest creature with its infinitely small particles on the other. Facing these infinities Pascal asks: "What then is man in nature after all? Nothing with regard to the infinite, a universe with regard to nothing, a medium between nothing and the universe, infinitely far from understanding the extremes. The end of things and their beginning are absolutely concealed from man in an impenetrable secret. He is equally incapable of conceiving the nothing from which he is drawn and the infinity by which he is devoured. "Hence heaven's way - as Lao-tse would say – has given and characterized the right pattern of behaviour and the right attitude, namely the modest position of man in the concert of the whole. We must just "empty" ourselves of false thoughts in order to achieve the right consciousness: consciousness of modesty.

> I have three treasures,
> Which I look after with love and care.
> The first is called sympathy;
> The second is called modesty;
> The third is called: not to strive to stand on top of the world.
> (Lao-tse)

What words unheard of in our ears today

Nowadays addiction to consumption, sex, drugs, power, and fame controls the scene. Everyone has become a prisoner of circumstances in one way or another; if not man himself then his children anyway. They are searching for their identity in externals. They sell their souls to just any slogan, status symbol and "brand articles"! Although material prosperity, luxurious consumption, and an extremely shallow and senseless subculture are no real cornerstones for a genuine personality. And never can true happiness be achieved through greed. Modesty makes rich says Saadi. "Modesty is indestructible wealth."[1] These were the words of Ali, the son-in-law of the Prophet (also handed down by

Mohammad). We find this wisdom of the Islamic world also confirmed in all other cultures.

> The wise man does not hoard.
> After having donated everything he owns to others,
> he still has more;
> After having given others everything he owns,
> his wealth is even greater.
> (Lao-tse)

On the contrary, the prophets of the technocratic materialistic order consider greed to be a "creative element, a virus of economic development" for man in the West and in the developing countries. On the banner of the Humane Society for which we stand, it is simply written "joy" (Freude, schöner Götterfunke – Joy, you purest spark divine - Schiller). Joy, however, has nothing to do with greed, wastefulness and an insatiable addiction to wealth. You cannot buy happiness with money – and everyone knows that!

Modesty – that's the source of genuine joy. But does modesty mean laziness and idleness? Not at all. Modesty means requiring the minimum while investing the maximum. A principle ranked above justice. The principle to reward everyone according to their spiritual and physical performance ensures justice which is the primary virtue of society! However, the principle of modesty also causes man to surpass himself, but first stations of self-finding are to be run through.

The ecological crisis which completely questions the future of our children underlines the truth of the Pascal laws today more than ever: that modesty is an essential fundamental value of human existence. Without it we will not only lose our souls in a fatal game against the externals but we will seriously endanger the conditions for our survival on earth. The principle of modesty is generally valid, it is true, but "rich nations" handle it differently than the "poor developing countries", where – with the exception of a thin upper class – millions and millions of people live in want while many rich people suffer from the consequences of superabundance.

Here we must optimize the reduction of production, organize consumption collectively, and return to a simple lifestyle through a general transformation of values without being victimized by "primitiveness" and technological stagnation; there, coupled with profound enlightenment, we must raise the living standard without opening the door to consumption fetishism. In the words of Dalai Lama the virtue of the wise man excels the midway between asceticism and indulgence: "I believe that it is also important for people who are not religious to free themselves from greed and become modest. He who does not know modesty, always yearns for more and more. Even if he owned the whole world, he wouldn't be satisfied... However, not only Buddhists but also Christian monks and nuns strive to lead a simple life in modesty. They also know that money, wealth, and fame cannot guarantee sustainable happiness. Therefore these things cannot become our ultimate goal."[2]

As already mentioned in the introduction the increase of world production will doubtlessly aggravate ecological crises. Even optimistic intellectuals do not exclude the collapse of nature as an inevitable consequence. It is obvious, isn't it, that this trend will not be without disastrous consequences for the equilibrium of the environment if more and more people keep wanting more and more. Currently two thirds of the world's population is anticipating the goal of reaching the living standard of the wealthy third in the industrial countries. If this occurs, the negative impact on the environment will certainly exceed two or three fold that of today. Hence the disaster is programmed.

But by whom? Surely not by those suffering from misery in the third world. Can we prevent those suffering people from searching for more happiness? The only reasonable remedy lies in changing the ways of thinking in the industrial nations and in redefining well-being. Hereby they should start from the central value of modesty and contentedness and not seek the characteristics of genuine development in "the investment sum for the working place", "income per head" or "growth rates".

"The distinction between 'developed' and 'developing' societies is not only inappropriate but also dangerously misleading as it considers the industrial societies to be already developed," says E. Laszlo.[3] The industrial countries have maneuvered the world into a precarious position. It is their responsibility to get us out of there. They should set up a humane order and take the lead with new examples. New ways of scientific findings and soft technologies will help with this reconstruction.

A materially modest life does not mean a relapse into primitiveness nor waiving progress; on the contrary, modesty will enable us to keep our spirit free for a stronger development of spirituality – a spirituality which will not put us into an arrogant and presumptuous mood, which will not seduce us to search for power and supremacy but lead us to Socratic wisdom so that we confess - in spite of all our knowledge - that we know nothing. This is a spirituality which leads to modesty according to the parable: The branch bearing more fruit bends even heavier down to earth.

---

1 The maxims of Imam Ali: *Nahdj al Balágha*

2 Dalai Lama: *Mitgefühl und Weisheit*, Herder Verlag

3 E. Laszlo: *Die inneren Grenzen der Menschheit*

# In Harmony with Nature

Humane naturalness together with natural humanity – this is the character of the new order, not based on violence, disguise, lies, fraud, self-deception, alienation, self-abandoning, self-denial, and banning love from interpersonal relations. What has happened to us? We have forgotten how to live because we have been taught to work… When we live we are outside of work, when we work, we don't live… We are exposed to powers which we ourselves have released… Money controls us and our happiness. Merchandise has managed to make us "human merchandise"… Spirits of the past take command over our present… Children are being domesticated and exposed to permanent violence, and thus they respond to this oppression with destruction and violence… Fears spooking in the jungle of the cities catch up with our fantasy and our own selves… The grey uniformity of incalculable uneasiness strangles and covers our sunrises… Hunger and malady reign in our world where piles of food and medicine perish in the warehouses of our metropolises… When we do a good deed, we make a negative impression, if we don't care, we are rewarded regularly… Benevolence, leniency, and sympathy are regarded as weakness… Imagination, subtleness disgrace us good-for-nothings…

We have to find again what we have lost: ourselves in nature and nature in ourselves! This is humane naturalness together with natural humanism! In other words: to understand each other in a sensitive way, to exist for one another for better or for worse and to help each other to surpass oneself – that is natural humanism. To perceive ourselves as a part of nature, to love nature instead of controlling it and to perform magic by creating the beautiful, the noble, the gentle and the intellectual – that is human naturalness.

The capitalistic alienated economic order cannot pay respect to the dogma that nature can, by all means, do without us while we cannot do without nature! Why? Because that economic system ignores the truth. This is expressed by an aphorism: somebody was sawing off the branch he was sitting on. The gardener saw him and shouted: "Stop or you'll fall with the sawed off branch!" But the thoughtless fellow had to continue turning his back to the truth because he needed some fuel for his fire. The capitalist economic order also sits with its back to the truth. The truth is that man should busy himself in order to enjoy a life in wealth and happiness but not to strive for profit as a goal in itself and not to pile up wealth and power. Wealth and power must - as we have repeatedly underlined – serve the people; otherwise they will be counterproductive and prevent people from freely pursuing happiness in life.

"Nature", said Ibn-Arabi, the greatest master of Islamic mystic, "is the touch of the Merciful; it has emerged from Him like breath from His mouth!" Spinoza said that nature was God and even added bravely that God was nature.

We will declare in the good tradition of the wise men of all peoples that the Divine is being and being is divine! However, if you turn your back to truth you will not only ignore your own divine descent but also the divinity of nature.

And this is exactly what is being practiced by the ruling technocratic materialism. For materialism nature is only a material source of profit and wealth. That's it! Capitalism is based on this misled order of values offering unscrupulously the divine unity of nature and mankind to its domineering god – capital - which craves power.

Also early socialism can be blamed for almost neglecting nature in spite of some beautiful assertions by Marx. Marx focused on the dialectics of mankind and nature when he referred to "humanizing nature and naturalizing mankind". At this point he certainly meant a vital mutual influence which was aimed at "the improvement of nature" on the one hand and the reconciliation of man and nature on the other. Nevertheless, there were theses and rules worked in the edifice of ideas of Marxism which prevented him from creating a splendid alternative to capitalism. One of these main theses referred to "productive forces". Marx's assumption that Communist paradise could only be implemented by means of an uninhibited omnilateral development of materialistic productive forces made the "improvement of nature" and the reconciliation of mankind and nature fall into oblivion during the further course of the Socialist regime. The craving to produce more and more, "the race against capitalism", the fatal attraction of merchandise whose possession seemed to make man worthy and respected, etc. and etc. made Socialism a destructive cogwheel machinery which confronted nature with hostility and hit it efficiently. No wonder! In a joint oeuvre of socialistic philosophers it was written: "The unity of nature exists in its materiality." This is far from the truth and has had devastating consequences for the destruction of the environment and the reduction of mankind.

The genuine divinity of existence is being denunciated and denied in order to elevate "material" to the throne of divinity! From now on only this "god" is being paid tribute to. In the future material will be worshiped exclusively. Commerce, consumption fetishism and technophility are the unavoidable consequences. The industrial nations are primarily responsible for the present environmental crises in this world. They have recklessly exploited and polluted the environment for decades and extinguished many living species. One hundred and fifty years ago with wise and simple words the Indian Chief Seattle warned the white man who was aggressively striving for domination: "The white man, temporarily in possession of power, already believes that he is God – possessing the earth. How can a man be the owner of his mother? Teach your children what we are teaching our children: the earth is our mother. What inflicts the earth also inflicts the sons of the earth. When man spits on the earth, he is spitting on himself. For everything is linked to each other… The earth is not owned by man but man is part of the earth…" [1]

Conscientious scientists of all nations are warning us about even worse consequences which may develop into disasters, catastrophes which we the people will encounter on this earth. Not only are plants and animals, the palatability of water, air and food seriously endangered, but the genes of men themselves are exposed to deformation and degeneration. These facts alone would be sufficient to convince any sensible person – capitalists included – of the hopeless dilemma of the present alienated "capitalistic system of values."

From this blind alley or trap mankind can only escape if there is global rethinking. Thanks to the courageous efforts of numerous alternatively thinking people this reorientation has already received an enormous thrust. The radical solution to the topical problems, however, will be possible in a Humane System where the primacy of ecology versus economy will be acknowledged in general and strictly obeyed. The Humane Economic System runs according to the value system of the following theses:
- preservation of the ecological balance,
- sustaining of species,
- keeping air, earth and water clean,
- wholesome nutrition for man and animals

Keeping these guiding principles without compromise requires:
- control of birth rate to avoid excessive growth of the world population
- adopting alternative soft technologies within industry
- supporting ecological farming
- changing people's habits and consumption behaviour by means of a new system of values

- recycling, reuse and multi-use of goods
- avoiding overproduction which only results in the waste and destruction of natural resources

Further complementary actions, above all the intensive international coordination of regional measures with the United Nations, are necessary to master the world-wide economical crisis.

---

1 Indian Chief Seattle. Speech to the President of the USA in 1855 – Walter Verlag (publishing house)

# The Principle of Solidarity

The doctrine of original sin is regarded by many philosophers as the initial idea of the solidarity of all mankind (1910, Raymond de Waha); others such as Heinrich Pesch – the founder of *solidaritism* in 1924 as a "system of mutual support" – regard the philosophy of the Middle Ages, especially the Christian perception of a God family comprising all mankind, as the principle of *solidaritism*. In Islam it was the term "Umma" which expressed the community of solidarity, in fact the brotherhood of all Muslims. Saadi von Schiraz crowned the idea of solidarity with the following verse:

> Adam's children are different members
> of one body of the one being.
> If the world inflicts pain on one of them,
> the others cannot rest.
> If you refuse to feel and know the suffering of others,
> you are not worthy to call yourself man.

"Society (the state) is not just a pile of atoms whose action and reaction benefit the whole mechanically by itself (individualism), nor is it a mechanism in a sense that the entire movement of all parts is caused by its direct or indirect contact with the center (socialism). It is much more 1.) an organism in which

a) An interior principle (authority) produces and preserves order and harmony for the benefit of the whole and according to this purpose, and where the different functions of life's processes find their optimal support in professional social organizations (organic development and unity),

b) Each single part appears in its development and for its own benefit through the other parts and their processes as well as conditioned by the whole and its welfare (real solidarity).

Society (the state) is 2.) an entity of moral, free beings (a moral organism).

a) With regard to man's eternal destiny the individual remains a purpose in himself. He enters society endowed with natural rights not necessarily derived from society but in need of society's acknowledgement and protection. He is a member of society but not only a member (sovereignty and self-responsibility).

b) The tie that links us together is moral obligation. Everyone appears to be connected in solidarity (common liability) with respect to the common benefit through obligations to justice and taking into account the welfare of fellow men."[1]

Solidarity, practically applied, serves the following functions:
- building a community
- protecting the community
- developing the community

The spirit of solidarity which infiltrates a community fulfills this function as human life itself strives for the fulfillment of joy and coping with misery. This principle of solidarity is also a cornerstone of the Humane Social System which we stand up for. It is a basic value not only for the future and the future forming of society but it is also our guideline for a humane way of living here and now! Our way of living is experienced solidarity, as it is in a way the fulfillment of joy and the execution of love. The basic values mentioned here may not be delegated timely or personally; the New Humanists themselves live according to these values!

From this point of view the principle of solidarity forms a way of living which cannot simply be put into a line with an organization principle. In the same way as man focuses on joy, he is dependent on partnership for the fulfillment of this expression of life. Solidarity has been laid into his cradle, so to speak. "Being man is an entity and this means that this is at the same time infinity implemented in a human way" (Nikolaus von Kues). Primarily, being man is experienced and likely learned within the family. Solidarity stands, as does joy itself, at the beginning. Conflicts from quarrel and hostility are of partial, incidental, and secondary nature. If the means and conditions for fulfilling were not scarce but abundantly available, the dimensions of quarrel would probably be limited and for the most part superfluous.

Life bubbles out of solidarity as from an inexhaustible source. Life from this source is of another quality than life stemming from quarrel and hostile discord. The latter stands in the realm of misery and obscurity. The former radiates in the light of joy and peace. Taking the side of the basic value of solidarity does not mean to close one's eyes to reality nor to negate the egoistic and adverse or the contentious and what breaks apart. It rather means only to accept one because of the other. Solidarity arises from the community in fate. If this community is questioned or threatened by conflicts, discord, hostilities, arrogance of rank, class interests, or contradictive dogmas then each member will strive to reconstruct the organic entity of those thrown together by fate as quickly as possible.

We, the New Humanists, are optimists with regard to the question "who whom?" i.e. we firmly believe that solidarity will be victorious in humanity, in the end and again and again. Otherwise those concerned will be lost and not survive. The human community as a living system is by all means capable of correcting disturbing factors and disharmony by itself and of reconstructing its entity in solidarity. Just in our world today many factors and conditions can be met which favorably influence solidarity internationally as well as within societies. Technological development enables modern communication world wide. World trade has brought the peoples of the world closer to each other to an extent never seen before. Ecological conditions make it clear that mankind can only continue to exist on the path of solidarity.

On the basis of the value concepts we have briefly explained above, we will now shortly turn towards discussing solidarity within society and within the world community. Of course the concept developed in the following is not a "must" but just food for further reflection and proposals:

"Digression"

## a – Within the social and economical realm

The Humane Social System of society which we stand up for is based on the principle of solidarity. With regard to domestic and foreign policy the Humane System is totally focused on solidarity. Once again we take up the doctrines and traditions of early socialism, Christian solidarity and national reforms which have left us an enormously rich theoretical and practical heritage. In the social economic area we now find the following rules and regulations as an expression of the solidarity community:

a-1: Control by the economy over the other areas of human activity and expressions of life is a one-dimensional orientation of society and must be rejected as "economism". Economism puts absolute priority on economy and subdues all actions of mankind to economical assessment. In the extreme case economism climaxes in materialistic determinism according to which the development of mankind is completely determined by the laws and processes of the economy. This is not only the prevailing idea (and also the dominating practice) in capitalism, but it also marked communism in the formerly socialistic countries. In these countries, it is true, contention with capitalism at the economic level took place, whereby the predominance of material over the spirit mercilessly asserted itself. The result was a perversion of socialism into state capitalism which was doomed to failure and had to lose the competition against the West because of the inertia of its bureaucracy. One of the most evil consequences of the economistic culture is the reduction of people to their jobs. Spiritual talents within the fields of art, science, sports, craftsmanship, family, and others were suppressed.

The solidaristic moment aspires to abolish this one-dimensionality and replace it by the development of work productivity on the one hand and a consciously modest life style on the other. In the words of Oswald von Nell-Breunning: "It will happen that an opinion which – I should say – we have regarded until now as an eternal category will prove to be a historical category, namely man's profession is the activity by which he makes his living. By increasing productivity the so-understood profession will really become triviality."[2] It is now necessary to reintegrate economy into the spiritual, moral, and historical life of society because man does not live by bread alone and is more than his profession!

a – 2: Capitalism means the reign of capital in politics, economy and culture. This reign is economically based on the exploitation of the working people by capital. Two ways to abolish capitalism have always existed: the violent revolutionary way to the total nationalisation of capital and the peaceful reform way which means severing the ties between capital and the power of the state and society.

We, the New Humanists, will continue to follow the second path keeping an eye on the negative but also the positive experience of the first path, for capital and free enterprise play a very important and – one might say – irreplaceable role during the innovation and development of societies. We must only be sure that capital remains and acts to serve all the people instead of a single class, whereby for the first time "coagulated, dead work" (Marx) reconciles with "living work." With the following and similar methods we will attempt to reach this goal of solidarity, detaching capital from the power of society and politics. This can only happen if we keep capital from dominating the following three areas:
- bureaucracy
- media
- political institutions such as political parties, etc.

A people without land has nothing to grow roots in. Thus the land (and everything above and below it) belongs to the people. Usufruct can only be acquired through lease, also from private persons and preferably by cooperatives.

All people possess the dwellings they inhabit. The landlords are reimbursed for the price of the dwellings.

The staff of every enterprise (banks, industry, insurance companies) will share the capital of the business by 49%.

Large businesses and economic units such as multinationals are decisively reduced and decartelized. The social engagement of capital is extended by law for research, donations, and sponsoring purposes, participation in "social costs" and new investments.

The Humane Market Economy distinguishes itself essentially from the free (liberal) market economy and the social market economy; in essence it is based on solidarity - solidarity and equilibrium between production and consumption whereby the market is governed by the people instead of the market governing the people. The Humane Market Economy structurally links three elements: the plan, statutory regulations and free competition.

Solidarity also signifies reducing the immense gap between present day wages and salaries in accordance with fairness.

People who are looking for work nowadays will not only receive care and job placement but also just unemployment support guaranteeing the essentials of life provided that there is proof of activity (in the household, caring for children, service in nursing homes and hospitals, further education, artistic and scientific activities, municipal improvement and maintenance, in different companies or self-employed). If voluntary activities are connected with income, the respective unemployed person will receive a bonus. In that way millions of hours of socially useful work merge on the one hand into the flow of the gross national product, and, on the other hand, those searching for work are socially integrated.

Health care, education, and pension are free of charge for everyone. The costs will be covered by the premiums of a general national insurance.

The military will be reduced to sheer defense purposes and its budget reduced to a minimum.

Those members of society who can neither work nor execute any activity will receive social help.

Women will receive equal wage for equal work. A mother and educator will get a special bonus and be given particular consideration and care at her working place and in her vocational career. A sound family is the natural breeding ground for love, solidarity, care, and consideration to thrive.

The principle of equality does not mean the distortion of woman into man; within the family woman plays a unique and irrevocable, caring, loving, and educational role which must not be abandoned. The family is the nucleus of solidarity which mainly grows in the love and serenity of mothers.

## b – Solidarity in the cultural area:

Just as the social and economic structure of the Humane Social System differs basically from capitalism and is based on joy, love, morality, and solidarity instead of profit maximizing, merciless competition and the spirit of profiteering, cultural life is obviously different and based on the humane values we have briefly indicated above. Precisely those people who are more or less spiritually busy and creative, in particular students, teachers, docents, theologians, scientists, researchers, inventors, technologists, journalists, intellectuals, artists, etc. will express humanity, solidarity, and emancipation in their creative spirit. They will be the social examples of the New Humanity for all other members and levels of society. They will criticize the capitalistic culture most precisely and make it clear to everybody that capitalism is not the climax of human history.

Not before overcoming the capitalistic culture will the way to even higher spiritual development phases be accessible. To criticize the capitalistic culture and to establish a humane, "solidaric and emancipatoric" culture – those are two historical tasks faced by the culture creating members of society. The culture creating have always fought tyranny, religious obscurantism, and social injustice. The culture creating have always implemented – step by step - the values of freedom and solidarity against servitude of any kind and the isolation of man. Now they are facing the colossal task of the second Enlightenment – which is an active one, i.e. it will only become a general imitation-worthy pattern for behavior if actively lived through a contagious and intensifying life style. In particular the following aspects can be mentioned which characterize a humane new culture:

The research and science of the New Human System must distinguish themselves fundamentally from the science and research of the capitalistic era, for the values on which they are respectively based have fundamentally different intentions and objectives.

The arts do not exist for the purpose of making one's mark, quenching the thirst for glory and profiteering, but rather for the spiritual uplifting and moral orientation of mankind. Sport and art are to bring a happy life to all mankind and serve to uplift their spirits in community.

A developed solidarity culture does not rise up arrogantly above the people and their culture; it just strives to be an offensive system and to participate constructively in other cultures. Openness towards and fruitful participation in the values of foreign cultures as well as mutual inspiration create a wonderful symbiosis and enormous enrichment.

In matters of belief the solidarity community will support tolerance, openness, the conformity of human nature, new forms of religiosity and the belief in God. The present day quarrel between the established religions implies disastrous consequences for the peace of mankind. It is the task of the courageous religious leaders and the theologians of those religions to actively engage themselves for the unity of divine nature and for religious peace in the world.

## c – Solidarity in the political area

The principle of solidarity penetrates the political infrastructure of the humane order of society like a guideline. The following concrete concepts will stimulate further discussions in detail:

Governing the people in solidarity. Present day governments characterized by the capitalistic culture are based upon dividing and isolating the people. The competitive struggle as a principle of democracy is being nourished here by the assumption that conflict is an integral part of man's nature. Everybody is thought to be striving with egoism for their advantage and to be forced into struggling against the others for survival. Contradiction, differences, and antagonism form the daily agenda and control political life where it is important to conquer and stabilize power. This is exactly what makes the unmistakable cultural assets of capitalism and helps it to tame or at least to keep in check the "wild and shrew" nature of man in consensus with democratic order.

We strictly refuse these moral concepts of mankind. In our opinion people do not primarily start out from conflicts and quarrels but from unity in solidarity for a life in joy, freedom, and peace. Hence we refuse a government as undemocratic which is only based on the feeble majority of a conflicting portion of the people. Such a government is not only undemocratic but also immoral. We suggest that in a "participatoric solidarity democracy" the governments emerging from the competition of political personalities, organizations, and parties ought to represent at least 75% of the votes of the people. This is not just a "grande coalition" or a kind of "government of national unity" temporarily formed now and then in order to cope with some time-limited and locally partial crises, but an institutionalized democratic form of government which is obliged to solidarism and emerges from its spirit.

A "solidarity council of the people" provides for the political leadership of the country. In democracies nowadays an ideal administrative body fails to make the longings, the requests, the interests, and the ideals of the people the subject of efficient political leadership. At present presidents, chancellors, and prime ministers carry out this office in their insecure hands, and this happens in a time when politics have assumed more and more complicated forms and involve complex contents. "The solidarity council of the people" consists of representatives from all vocational  groups, unions and associations, parties, confessions, organizations for women and youth as well as delegates of those parties which have failed to become members of the legislative organ since they have missed the 5% clause. Directives and guidelines for the political leadership of a country to be periodically recommended to the government emerge from summarizing public conversations, discussions and elaborated statements in the council.

Freeing society from bureaucracy is not only a tactically and time-wise limited matter in participatoric solidarity democracy but it is a permanent attitude and a lasting institution which executes respective tasks by means of a special tool. Membership in this organ to break away from bureaucracy is voluntary. Among others this organ has to undertake the following and similar steps:

- Keep the influence of bureaucracy away from legislation.
- Show vigilance when executing laws so that they are not undermined and perverted by bureaucracy.
- Break down the resistance of bureaucracy when alterations are necessary.
- Reduce the number of civil servants.
- Make civil servants subject to notice.
- Ensure the transparency of the decisions of the authorities.
- Execute public relations in each office of the ministries and in enterprises.
- Simplify directives and rules and regulations for civil servants.
- Accelerate the implementation of measures demanded by the citizens.
- Battle against bureaucracy and red tape.
- Implement the periodic exchange of ministerial civil servants.

Democratizing social areas:

For participatoric solidarity democracy the term democracy is far reaching and covers all areas of life, not only politics. Above all, the following institutions must undergo a process of democratizing;

a) The family: in humane solidarity democracy democratic principles such as liberty and equality are to form a fruitful symbiosis with parental authority.

b) In schools and universities education, vocational training, teaching, and research must proceed in a democratic-solidarity spirit and ensure that the offspring will be courageous, competent, and liberally thinking and will merge in the spirit of solidarity.

c) In humane solidarity democracy the presently prevailing formally democratic conduct in companies and enterprises, in clubs and associations, in parties and in the media will be replaced by a genuine democratic spirit and conduct. Whoever proclaims democracy must not be blind to the fact that open and concealed oligarchies, hierarchies, and bureaucratic power structures reign to a large extent in the organizations mentioned.

d) Citizens' participation in their social life – that is in one word the soul of the solidarity humane democracy of the future. At present democratic elections serve as an alibi and pretend sovereignty of the people. In reality, however, the centers of power are being occupied by opinion builders and media owners, by the financiers of parties and lobbies, by the administrators of religions and by patriarchs, by multinational corporations and by the chief executive offices of leading industry and commerce, by houses of nobility and by their rulers ....

The narrowly meshed network of positive law:

In the past positive law has played a certain progressive role in the sense that it introduced the rule of law. Today, however, society risks not only suffocating in waste but also in huge piles of positive law.  Bullied and helpless the masses face blind *Justitia* while the simple people are the real losers of litigation. Solidarity and humane democracy attempts to terminate this intolerable situation by means of the following and similar measures:

- Simplify the legal system.
- Streamline legal proceedings free of charge.
- Generally revive traditional arbitration in quarters, businesses, families, etc.
- Create extensive areas not regulated by law for the citizens by the abolishment of legal clauses which hinder the uninhibited settlement between people and which force people into the straightjackets of legal standards.

With the proliferation of the spirit of love and solidarity among people there will be morality which will make laws superfluous for the most part. Humane democracy is founded on the rule of law it is true but it is not a system of dogmatism and growing and endless free-for-all litigation. Here the spirit of forgiving and reconciliation sets the tone. This reigning culture is all about solidarity instead of litigation and dispute!

Solidarity in the world's community of peoples and countries:

"Solidarity as a principle is basically internationally valid. The interest of the individual in the welfare of the whole within human society cannot be restricted to one state's society. The principle of solidarity is also valid for the community which represents itself as a structured association of historically founded single states – without being a (world) stately society itself. International solidarity exists in a comprehensive way, because those states – in so far as they are to be regarded as individuals – are linked with mutual impact to each other politically, economically, socially, yes, absolutely in their entire nature as organizations conditioned by culture."[3]

The dream of all humanists and socially thinking people has been to achieve a harmonious, peaceful, and well-functioning world union of mankind far from all national, ethnic, denominational, racial, and state borders. The United Nations is only one milestone along this path to the future; many more steps, many more milestones will be necessary to finally implement that bold dream of world unity of mankind in a federal world state. Fortunately many positive and, alas, also negative circumstances have contributed to bringing us closer to the above goal. Those factors comprise: technological progress, economic interconnections, the vivid cultural interaction of peoples, encouraging political reasons and institutions, and, last but not least, the ecological necessity to remember across national and state borders that the earth is Mother Nature of all mankind. All these circumstances have led to an awareness boom of mankind's world unity in peace and liberty, which we can only approve of. The New Humanists pursue with vigilance these supporting and inhibiting parameters of growing solidarity among the world's populations. We have set up targets near and far and therefore also priorities, in particular the following:

- A peaceful struggle in solidarity against any imperial, hegemonic, and neo-colonial totalitarian allures in the world.
- Solidarity with the peoples suffering under handed down forms of power and dictatorships.
- Support to underdeveloped countries so they can develop by their own power and abolish the roots of poverty, misery, and backlog.
- Support of just world trade which has to be structured and managed democratically.
- Solidaric efforts of all forces for peace and disarmament - for peace is the ripe fruit of the spirit of solidarity.
- Indestructible solidarity with all peoples and states for the general protection of the environment and for the salvation of the earth.
- The United Nations, human rights, and international law are to be efficient and supporting levers to unify and integrate peoples and states of the earth.
- One state for one world instead of the whole world for one state (= globalization).

Finally Rudolf Diesel, the inventor of the diesel engine, should be mentioned as one of the first representatives of the idea of solidarity. He firmly believed that this idea would eliminate the misery of the socially weak and "liberate" them from their heavy burden. In 1903 he already regarded solidarism as the motor "to a great, free and genuine humanity, to a new form of culture which would enhance mankind's means enormously."[4]

1       Heinrich Pesch, *Solidarität als Pflicht*, 1925

2       Oswald von Nell-Breunning, *Arbeitet der Mensch zu viel?*, 1985

3       Rudolph Diesel, *Solidarismus, natürliche wirtschaftliche Erlösung des Menschen*, München 1903

4       Rudolf Fleck, *Wirtschaftlicher Solidarismus*

# Epilogue

In a few modest words we have now expressed our yearnings concerning the future of our children and our own lives, individually and within the community. Hereby we lean on the statements of the wise men of the world who have again and again emphatically expressed the same values and paths. In addition, we strive to base our thoughts on three standpoints from which we describe them:

- infinity
- eternity
- "from the heart of mankind"

Let us make one last remark characterizing our way of living which is, in fact, identical to our "active enlightenment" in an unmistakable way: We tread a peaceful path without violence but with firm steps and clear concepts. We have taken on this peaceful path without violence with Lao-tse from the "Way of Heaven". Violence creates violence. And this is exactly what we refuse for it is not heaven's way. Heaven's way is one of peace and reconciliation. Tao is the soft element which defeats the hard, just as water patiently erodes the rock. Like Christ we even love our "enemies", for love heals the hostile heart infected with hatred. But will power give in without contra-power? If our silence speaks volumes, if our heart's pulse beats in our steps, if we live joyfully and if we love the life of other's just as our own, if we choose non-desire as desire, if we remain on the earth but wander along the path of the divine whole when deeds follow our beliefs, then you may call this "contra-power" a contra-power, it is true, that dissolves into nothing as soon as it has devoured power. We want to revolutionize society without provoking a revolution.

New Humanism is an interminable process of becoming and a permanent commitment to the ideas and ideals described in this book. An ideal will not implement itself technically but organically. It is the result of lively growth. We are living with our ideals and our ideals live with us and through us. This is how the future Humane System shall be filled with life and demonstrated here and now, so that the future has a chance to sprout from the present seeds. New Humanism is essentially a humane alternative way of living in which we unleash the convincing power of a better example, a way of living in peace and love with unilaterally open spirituality. Hence New Humanism is more than a new political party. Every political party is the twofold expression of partitions, whereas New Humanism is the requirement and the action of all mankind and the universality of the humane. It is the integrating power within society and worldwide and the climax of divergent powers, which are called upon to reconcile, to reflect and to show solidarity.

Present day primates of the state as well as of the economy are each the embodiment of the reign of one part over the whole. The partial is a component of life, it is true, but not life itself. We strive for life! The human spirit is a diamond with countless facets. The bigger the stone and the more beautiful the cutting, the more splendid and unique the brilliance. This is what we are particularly focusing upon. This is what we are taken up in! But our liberty does not always consist of doing what we can do but also of doing what we are to do, even if this sometimes implies painful renunciation. Different religions are only different ways of perceiving the divine truth which every individual without a veil in the heart can become aware of. We are the permanent search for this truth without being a new religion or giving our consent to an existing religion which has ceased to keep on searching. The Humane System of the future can only be a system of peace – peace among people and peace in the hearts of mankind. We are the joyful message of a peaceful morning. Everything in this world is linked. Hence at the same time we are the tears of joy and sighs of the tortured creature! As long as the echo of our women's serene laughter sounds in heaven's sphere, as long as the heavy night of pains lasts, our unredeemed hope for the bright morning of salvation will prevail. Back-to-nature does not mean returning to primitiveness, for nature itself is the source of all spirituality. Back-to-nature is the justified call for the preservation of nature, for a life in harmony with nature and in beautiful, genuine naturalness. The right path, that's the heavenly way; we have chosen this path as our goal with thinking hearts and sensitive brains …

www.ingramcontent.com/pod-product-compliance
Lightning Source LLC
Chambersburg PA
CBHW081420090426
42738CB00017B/3430